HAPPILY EVER CRAFTER

ONCE UPON A

DINOSAUR CRAFT

ANNALEES LIM

Lerner Publications ◆ Minneapolis

First American edition published in 2020 by Lerner Publishing Group, Inc.

First published in Great Britain in 2018 by Wayland
Copyright © Hodder and Stoughton, 2018
All rights reserved.

Senior Commissioning Editor: Melanie Palmer
Design: Square and Circus
Illustrations: Supriya Sahai

Additional illustrations: Freepik

Lerner Publications Company
A division of Lerner Publishing Group, Inc.
241 First Avenue North
Minneapolis, MN 55401 USA

For reading levels and more information, look up this title at www.lernerbooks.com.

Main body text set in Billy Infant Regular 17/24.
Typeface provided by SparkyType.

Library of Congress Cataloging-in-Publication Data

The Cataloging-in-Publication Data for *Once Upon a Dinosaur Craft* is on file at the Library of Congress.
ISBN 978-1-5415-5881-6 (lib. bdg.)
ISBN 978-1-5415-6194-6 (eb pdf)

Manufactured in the United States of America
1-46270-46262-11/12/2018

SAFETY INFORMATION:
Please ask an adult for help with any activities that could be tricky or involve cooking or handling glass. Ask adult permission when appropriate.

CONTENTS

DINOSAURS

For millions of years dinosaurs ruled the earth. They lived on every continent and in different terrains and climates, constantly evolving to suit their changing environments.

The word dinosaur comes from the Greek word for "terrible lizard," but this does not mean that all dinosaurs were big and scary. While a lot of sharp-clawed dinosaurs were carnivores (meat-eaters), there were many more dinosaurs that were herbivores (plant-eaters). You can tell which ones these were by looking for their blunt hooves or scale-like toenails.

FACT!
Some scientists believe that many dinosaurs had feathers, including *Tyrannosaurus rex*. The closest living relative to the dinosaur is the chicken!

A paleontologist is a person who finds and studies fossils to learn more about dinosaurs and how they lived. When you see dinosaur skeletons in museums, you aren't actually looking at real bones—they're fossils. This special type of rock replaces bone over a long period of time and makes an exact replica in its place.

TOP TIP

With this book you can make lots of discoveries and learn more about dinosaurs. Make fun crafts using materials you find around your house, then dress up in costumes and plan the best dino party in town. All of these projects are easy to follow, but ask an adult for help if you need it!

No one really knows what dinosaurs looked like because we only have their bones to study. When using this book, use your imagination to create the most unique-looking dinosaurs. Use lots of different colors—maybe even try adding feathers to your creations!

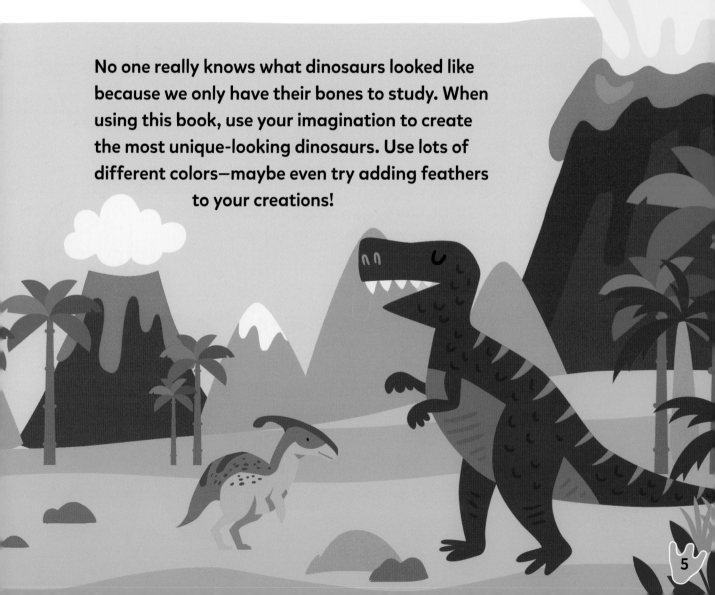

BIG BEASTS, DINO DRESS

Recycle old pieces of clothing and transform them into dinosaur costumes. These prehistoric projects are easy to make, but you can add your own designs too. Try mixing different materials together, changing colors, or combining projects to create a brand-new dinosaur.

SPINOSAURUS SPINE

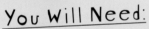

Spinosaurus is one of the largest and longest dinosaurs ever to roam the earth. These carnivores had a long face with a large bone fin on their back called a sail. They lived both on the land and in the sea, just like crocodiles do, and mainly ate fish.

You Will Need:
- CARDBOARD • SCISSORS • PENCIL
- PAINT • CARDSTOCK
- GLUE STICK • PAINTBRUSH
- RIBBON OR STRING

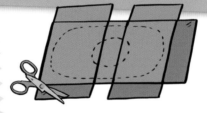

1. Flatten out a large cardboard box and cut it into a long oval shape with a hole in the middle.

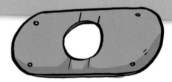

2. Make four small holes on the edges of the oval shape.

3. Cut out a half circle sail and a triangle tail shape. Glue these to one half of the oval.

4. Stick a small strip of L-shaped cardstock to either side of the circle sail.

5. Paint the whole thing and let it dry before threading ribbon or string through the holes.

TRICERATOPS HEADDRESS

Triceratops is a large four-legged dinosaur with a frill made from bone around its head. Its name means "three-horned face" because it has one horn on its nose and two on the top of its head. The horns were used for defense rather than hunting, since they were herbivores.

1. Cut out a crescent shape from some scrap cardstock, making sure you have five small triangle shapes on top.

2. Bend this over the top of the hat, slightly closer to the back, and staple it in place at the sides.

You Will Need:
- AN OLD BASEBALL CAP
- CARDSTOCK • SCISSORS
- TAPE • STAPLER • NEWSPAPER
- GREEN/BLACK/WHITE TISSUE PAPER • WHITE CRAFT GLUE

3. Scrunch up bits of newspaper and stick them onto the hat to add details to the frill and make eyes and a nose.

4. Make three cones from semicircles of cardstock and tape them onto the cap in a triangle formation.

5. Cover the whole thing with layers of green, black, and white tissue paper and white craft glue. Leave to dry in a warm place before wearing.

EUOPLOCEPHALUS TAIL

Euoplocephalus was a herbivore and had large plates covering its body like armor. It had spikes all over its body and would swing its long tail with a boulder-shaped hammer at the end to defend itself from predators.

You Will Need:

- AN OLD PAIR OF PANTS
- NEEDLE AND THREAD • NEWSPAPER
- RUBBER BANDS • PAPER • SCISSORS
- WHITE CRAFT GLUE

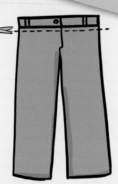

1. Cut the waistband off some pants and separate the legs.

2. Sew one of the legs onto the waistband and stuff with scrunched up newspaper.

3. Put the other pants leg inside to make a long tail and secure it with a rubber band.

4. Stuff the top section of the second pants leg with more stuffing and hold in place with a rubber band. Cut off the excess pants leg.

5. Decorate the tail with paper spikes stuck on with glue.

PTERODACTYLUS WINGS

People often mistakenly call all winged reptiles pterodactyls, but the word for this group of creatures is pterosaurs. One of the most recognized members of the group is *Pterodactylus*. Its name means "winged finger" because it has bat-like wings.

1. Cut the body section off the T-shirt.

2. Open up the fabric by cutting along one side. Then cut diagonally so that it makes two triangles.

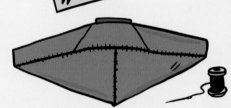

3. Glue or stitch the fabric triangles onto each sleeve. Make two paper feet and stick them to the bottom of the wings.

4. Paint your costume using fabric paints or markers.

What do you call a dinosaur who knows lots of words?

A Thesaurus!

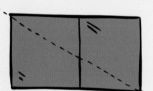

PREHISTORIC PARTY PLANNING

The best birthday bashes and holiday celebrations don't organize themselves. They can take weeks of planning, but it's all worth it to see your excited guests enjoying themselves. Follow these top tips and reminders to help you plan an epic Jurassic-themed party.

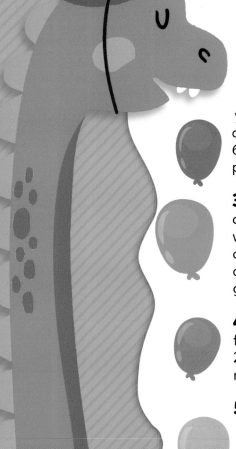

KEEP A LIST
Write down everything you will need to do for the party. Give yourself plenty of time to prepare, especially if you have big plans to decorate, bake, and build. Mark your to do list with a dinosaur sticker or draw a big dino footprint alongside each task to show when you've done it.

1. Land of the dinosaurs: Transport your guests back in time millions of years by creating the perfect dino habitat. There are plenty of ideas on page 16 to transform your party space.

2. Dino dress up: If your party has a theme, you might want to ask your guests to wear fancy outfits too. Find some costume projects on page 6 for inspiration. You can always make extras and put them in a box so people can try them on.

3. Play some games: Roaring and stomping around like dinosaurs can be great fun, especially when you're playing games. The projects on page 12 all have a dino theme and can be made beforehand or as a fun party activity for you to entertain your guests with.

4. Ferocious food: Make sure you have plenty of food ready to feed your monstrous gang. Turn to page 20 for simple recipes to keep everyone's stomach from roaring and rumbling.

5. Triassic trinkets: On page 24 you will find lots of mini crafts that are perfect to add to your decorations, give out as thank-you gifts, or to award as prizes for the best dressed dinosaurs at the party.

INVITATIONS

Some of the most important things to remember are the invitations. Send one to everyone you want to invite and make sure to tell them all the information they need. Use this dinosaur themed invitation as a template to make your own.

What: Let everyone know why you are celebrating.

To: Invite your best prehistoric pals to the party.

You are invited to my BIRTHDAY PARTY . . .

To: _____
Where: _____
When: _____
Dress code: _____
RSVP: _____

When and Where: Write the date, address, and time of the party.

Dress code: What would you like everyone to wear?

RSVP: Ask people to let you know if they can come.

PARTY GAMES

These four party projects are all made from things you will find around the house. By recycling and reusing things, you are saving money and being environmentally friendly. You can ask friends or neighbors if they have any of the things you need too.

THE BIG DIG

Paleontologists study dinosaurs by looking at their fossils. There are lots of places all around the world where you can look for fossilized bones and new types of dinosaurs. You have to be very careful not to damage the fossils you excavate by using tools like shovels and brushes.

You Will Need:

- TIN FOIL • PAPER TOWEL
- WHITE CRAFT GLUE • PAPER
- COLORED MARKERS

1. Mold the tin foil into bone shapes. You will need five for each person playing the game.

2. Cover each bone with a layer of paper towel and craft glue. Leave to dry.

3. Draw a colored spot on each bone with the markers. Each set of bones should be a different color.

4. Draw a dinosaur shape on a piece of paper. Make one for each player.

HOW TO PLAY

Scatter the bones into the bottom of a large container or wading pool and cover with a layer of sand. Decide who is going to collect which color and place a dino sheet on the floor for each player. At the start, everyone runs toward the dig and uses their paintbrush to brush off the sand and reveal the bones. Once you have found your color of bone, run back to the start and place the bone on the sheet. Then run back to find another bone. The winner is the person who finds all five of their bones the fastest.

DINO HUNT

Why didn't the T. rex get asked to play baseball?

He was a 'saur loser!

Did you know that different dinosaurs lived at different periods of time called the Triassic, Jurassic, and Cretaceous? This means that some of the dinosaurs you've heard of never lived alongside each other. *Tyrannosaurus rex* would never have met *Stegosaurus*, and *Iguanodon* would never have seen *Triceratops*.

You Will Need:

- PAPER TOWEL TUBE • PAPER
- SCISSORS • TAPE
- STRING • COLORED CARDSTOCK
- DRY ERASE MARKER

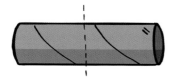

1. Cut the kitchen roll tube in half and cover each with some paper.

2. Stick the two tubes together with tape.

3. Tape some string to the sides of the tube to make the binoculars. Make one pair for each player.

4. Cut out colored dinosaur shapes from the cardstock.

5. Tape a loop of string to each one.

HOW TO PLAY

Write a letter on each dinosaur so that it spells a word. Hang up the letters in a tree or on the branches of a bush. Players who do not know what the word is use their binoculars to find the letters. The first person to unscramble the letters and shout out the correct word wins!

T. REX RAMPAGE

Tyrannosaurus rex was a large and powerful carnivore that had a big head, small arms, and a long tail to help it balance. Most lived in North America. Evidence of their existence was first found in 1874 in Golden, Colorado. But it wasn't until 1900 that the first nearly complete skeleton was discovered. The T. rex was officially named two years later.

You Will Need:

- CONSTRUCTION PAPER • STAPLER
- WHITE PAPER • MARKERS
- SCRAP FABRIC

1. Make a circle out of construction paper that fits around your head.

2. Staple two more strips of paper to the front.

3. Glue some white triangle teeth onto the strips of paper.

4. Draw on some eyes with a marker.

5. Cut out a triangle shape from some fabric. This will be the tail. Make a T. rex set for each player.

HOW TO PLAY

Everyone wears their own hat and tucks the triangle tail into the back of their waistband. When the game starts, everyone needs to try and grab the tails from the backs of the other players. If your tail is taken, you are out. The winner is the last person to have their tail still tucked in.

FEED THE DINOSAUR

Paleontologists can tell a lot about how a dinosaur lived by what sort of teeth it had. Some had rows and rows of sharp teeth and some had smaller, flatter teeth. This shows whether they ate mostly meat or mostly plants.

You Will Need:

- LARGE CARDBOARD BOXES
- GLUE STICK • WHITE PAPER
- SCISSORS • PAINT • PAINTBRUSH
- NEWSPAPER

1. Cut a hole from the front of the box.

2. Stick white triangles inside the hole.

3. Decorate the box with more cardboard to make a head, eyes, a nose, and horns.

4. Paint the box in different colors and leave to dry.

5. Scrunch up pieces of paper or newspaper into balls and put them in a pile.

HOW TO PLAY

See how many balls of newspaper you can throw into the dinosaur's mouth in 60 seconds. Take turns and keep your scores written down to see who is the ultimate winner.

PARTY DECORATIONS

Decorating a room can be a fun, quick, and simple way to set the scene and get everyone in the party mood. Hang things from the ceiling, cover tables and chairs, and even replace paintings and photographs with your own hangings— just be sure to ask an adult first!

IN THE JUNGLE

In the age of the dinosaurs, there were no buildings or roads, so the landscape looked very different from today. During the Jurassic period the weather was often wet and warm, which was an ideal environment for lots of green plants and tall trees to grow.

You Will Need:

- WATERED-DOWN GREEN PAINT
- NEWSPAPER
- PENCIL • PAINTBRUSH
- STRING • SCISSORS
- TAPE

1. Paint the sheets of newspaper with the green paint and leave to dry.

2. Fold the sheets in half and draw half a fern shape on each one. Cut the shapes out.

3. Gather the fern leaves together in a bunch around a length of string.

4. Wrap some tape around the bunch and hang it up.

BARYONYX BONES

Baryonyx means "heavy claw." This dinosaur had a very large claw on each thumb. It was first discovered in a clay pit in 1983 in Surrey, England, and the original fossil can still be seen at the Natural History Museum in London.

You Will Need:
- CARDSTOCK • MASKING TAPE
- SCISSORS • YOGURT CONTAINER
- BROWN CRAYON

1. Cut out two claw shapes from some cardstock.

Where did Stegosaurus go shopping?
The Dino-Store!

2. Tape these to the edges of a small yogurt container.

4. Rub the surface lightly with a brown crayon. Color the base a darker brown by pressing harder with the same crayon.

3. Use more masking tape to join the sides of the claw together!

TYRANNOTITAN TEETH

A *Tyrannotitan* skeleton was only discovered in 2005 on a farm in Argentina in South America. It was a fierce carnivore that had about sixty teeth in its giant jaw and was one of the main predators of its time.

You Will Need:
- LIGHTWEIGHT PAPER
- TWO BALLOONS • TAPE
- PAPER • SCISSORS

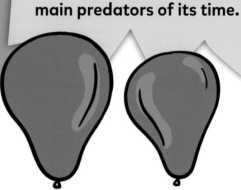

1. Blow up two balloons, one slightly bigger than the other.

2. Stick them to each other with tape.

3. Make some paper arms, legs, and a tail. Cut them out and stick them onto the balloon.

4. Cut out zigzags from some black paper. Discard the edges and keep the leftover piece of paper.

TOP TIP
If you rub the balloon onto your sweater, the static electricity will stick it to the ceiling.

5. Tape this paper onto the balloon and add eyes.

TROODON EGGS

Troodon was one of the smaller dinosaurs, measuring up to just 35 inches in height. It laid around twenty eggs over a period of about a week in small clusters on the ground. Scientists believe that the eggs were kept warm by the adult sitting on them rather than the eggs being buried in the ground.

You Will Need:

- TWO WATER BOTTLES WITH ROUND BOTTOMS • POLYSTYRENE
- WHITE CRAFT GLUE
- PAPER TOWEL • TAPE

1. Cut two water bottles in half.

2. Tape the two bottom halves together using tape.

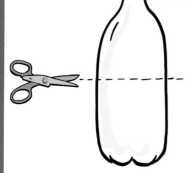

3. Break up some chunks of polystyrene and mix in some glue.

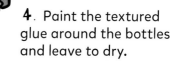

4. Paint the textured glue around the bottles and leave to dry.

5. Tear the paper towel into pieces and stick a layer on top of the bottles using the white craft glue.

TOP TIP

Use these as decorations for the table. Write your guests' names on them so they know where to sit. Or, scatter them in the middle to make a centerpiece.

PARTY FOOD

Research suggests that dinosaurs swallowed large rocks to help things digest better in their stomach, but you won't need any stones to help your guests enjoy these recipes! Remember to wash your hands before cooking, and always ask an adult for help using the oven or sharp knives.

DINO NESTS

You Will Need:
- GRANOLA BARS • MILK CHOCOLATE
- DARK CHOCOLATE CHIPS
- DRIED CHERRIES • PAPER BOWL
- CLING WRAP

It is hard to find fossilized dinosaur nests, so we don't know for sure what they looked like. But as scientists learn more about the link between dinosaurs and birds, it is becoming more likely that many species of dinosaurs used open nests in the ground to look after their young.

1. Break up some granola bars into a bowl.

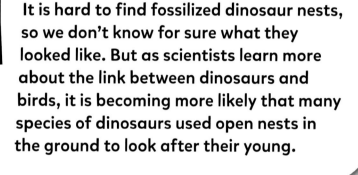

2. Melt a milk chocolate bar and pour it into the cereal. Add some dark chocolate chips and dried cherries into the mixture and mix well.

TOP TIP

Add chocolate eggs to the nest to complete. You could always add some gummy lizards to look like some have just hatched.

3. Line a paper bowl with cling wrap.

4. Spoon the mixture into the bowl and press into the sides to make a nest shape. Leave to cool before removing from the bowl.

ICE AGE MERINGUES

There have been five major ice ages where the earth's temperature lowers and the polar ice caps grow larger, covering more of the planet in ice and glaciers. Did you know that we are actually in an ice age right now? It is in the warmer period between intense freezes. This warmer period could last for thousands of years, and the ice age could last for millions of years!

You Will Need:
- MERINGUE NESTS
- VANILLA ICE CREAM
- LEMON CURD • COCONUT

1. Crush up some meringue nests in a bowl.

2. Slightly soften the vanilla ice cream and add to the meringues. Mix well.

3. Spread a spoonful of lemon curd on top of a meringue nest.

4. Add a scoop of the ice cream mixture on top of the lemon curd.

5. Sprinkle some coconut on top.

LAVA-LY VOLCANO BREAD

Volcanoes are usually formed in mountains. They act like a vent so the magma and gas that's built up underneath the earth's surface can escape. There are many all over the planet. Most are extinct, meaning they will not erupt. Some are dormant, which means they could erupt in the future. Others are active, so you are likely to see lava flowing out of them.

You Will Need:

- OVENPROOF BOWL • SMALL OVENPROOF BOWL • BAKING TRAY
- PARCHMENT PAPER • PIZZA DOUGH • GRATED CHEESE
- TOMATO SALSA

1. Place an ovenproof bowl and a smaller ovenproof bowl onto a baking tray.

2. Cover this with a sheet of parchment paper, making sure you make an indent at the top.

3. Roll out the pizza dough and place on top of the parchment paper. Sprinkle with cheese.

BAKE!

4. Bake until golden brown.

5. Serve with a tomato salsa dip in the top.

MARSHMALLOW MEGALOSAURUS

Megalosaurus was a large two-legged dinosaur with two short arms and three sharp claws on each hand. When it was first discovered people thought it was a part of an old elephant because no one knew about dinosaurs then.

You Will Need:

- CRUSHED CHOCOLATE COOKIES
- BAKING TRAY • SMALL AND LARGE MARSHMALLOWS • DARK CHOCOLATE
- ICING PENS

1. Fill a baking tray with crushed chocolate cookies.

2. Melt some dark chocolate—this will act like your glue.

3. Make the head and hips from three large marshmallows. Place them into the crushed cookies.

4. Use mini marshmallows to make the spine, tail, ribs, arms, and legs. Join it all together by pouring in the melted chocolate.

5. Use an icing pen to add more details to the head and claws.

CRAFT-O-SAURUS

Gather together all your craft materials and get to work. These projects will fit in well with your other party preparations—or you can just make them for fun. Cover surfaces before you start to keep things from getting messy and remember to clean up afterward.

PLATEOSAURUS PLATES

Plateosaurus is one of the earliest dinosaurs to have roamed the earth. It was a two-legged plant eater that had a long neck with a small head. Its name means "flat lizard." Lots of fossils of this dinosaur have been discovered. Scientists believe that they used to live in herds.

You Will Need:
- PAPER PLATE • GREEN PAINTS
- PAINTBRUSH OR SPONGE • PENCIL
- SCISSORS • TAPE • MARKERS

1. Paint a paper plate in different shades of green. Try using a sponge to add some texture.

2. Draw a body, head, tail, arms, and legs in parts onto the plate.

3. Cut them out and arrange in the right order.

4. Stick them together by overlapping the edges and taping the back.

5. Draw on details to the face and to the body.

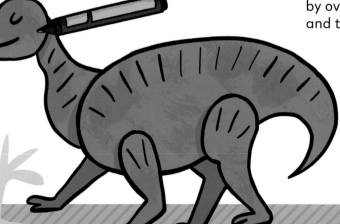

CARNOTAURUS

Carnotaurus means "meat-eating bull." It is thought to be one of the fastest dinosaurs. It had a very textured and bumpy body and would use the two horns on the side of its head to hunt and fight. Its arms were so small that they would not have been very useful at all.

You Will Need:
- TWO SHEETS OF SANDPAPER
- COLORED CRAYONS • GLUE STICK
- BLUE PIECE OF PAPER

1. Color one sheet of sandpaper using a green crayon.

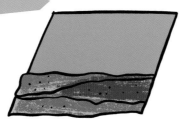

2. Tear up half the green into strips and glue it onto the bottom of a blue piece of paper to make a landscape.

3. Tear the other half of the green sheet into leaf shapes and stick them around the edge.

4. Draw the Carnotaurus on another piece of sandpaper using more crayons and roughly tear it out.

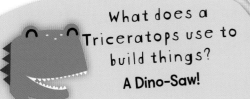

What does a Triceratops use to build things?
A Dino-Saw!

5. Stick the dinosaur into the scene with glue.

FOSSILS

Fossils are any animal or plant remains that are over 100,000 years old. They can be as small as shells and insects or as big as giant dinosaurs. The word "fossil" comes from the Latin word for "dug up." The most common fossils are ammonites, which can be found on beaches all around the world.

1. Draw a circle on a piece of cardboard using a roll of tape and cut it out.

You Will Need:
- CARDBOARD • SCISSORS • WHITE CRAFT GLUE
- DRIED PASTA • GRAY PAINT • PAINTBRUSH

2. Spread a layer of glue over the cardboard circle.

3. Use different shapes of pasta to create a spiral.

5. Cover with a thin layer of white craft glue and leave to dry.

4. Paint the pasta a dark gray color and leave to dry.

VOLCANO

We don't know exactly why the dinosaurs went extinct 65 million years ago. Scientists believe it could be because a giant asteroid hit the earth, or that a large volcano erupted and changed the earth's climate so much that it was hard for any living thing to survive.

You Will Need:

- TWO PLASTIC CUPS • GLUE STICK
- TAPE • GREEN CARDSTOCK
- BROWN, YELLOW, RED, AND ORANGE PAPER • SCISSORS

1. Cover one plastic cup with brown paper. Glue this onto some green cardstock.

2. Cover another plastic cup in red paper.

3. Cut the top so that it is wavy.

4. Add layers of orange and yellow paper with wavy edges. Place them behind the red paper.

5. Stick this onto the top of the brown cup and secure by wrapping a strip of brown paper around where they touch.

WOOLLY BRACHIOSAURUS

Brachiosaurus was a sauropod, which means it had a long neck and tail but a small head. It grew to be as tall as three school buses stacked on top of each other. Like giraffes, it ate from tall trees.

1. Cut into each end of one long cardboard tube so the edges are at an angle.

2. Make one of the short cardboard tubes smaller than the other. Then cut triangles into the tops of each tube.

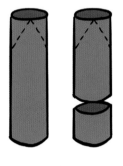

3. Cut the last short tube in half and then cut triangles into one end.

4. Stick the tubes together using the masking tape.

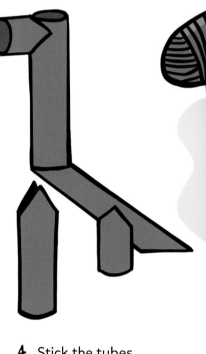

5. Cover with glue and start winding the yarn around the tubes until it is all covered. Glue the googly eyes on.

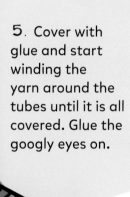

ICHTHYOSAURUS
PAPER SCULPTURE

You Will Need:
- LIGHT AND DARK BLUE PAPER
- TAPE • SCISSORS • MARKERS

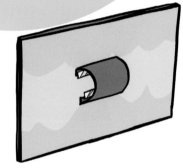

Ichthyosaurus is Greek for "fish lizard," which correctly describes this species of reptile that once lived in the water. Unlike fish, they needed to breathe air. Their appearance was similar to a dolphin, although they actually had more in common with land mammals.

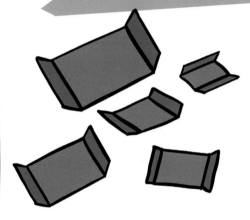

1. Cut out five rectangles, each one smaller than the one before. Fold each rectangle twice so that they look like they have two flaps.

2. Take the largest rectangle and tape it to the middle of a piece of paper.

3. Put tape on the other flap, bend into an arch, and stick down. Repeat with the other rectangles.

4. Cut out some fins and a tail and stick them onto the rectangles.

5. Add an eye and mouth using a marker.

29

AMBER INSECTS

Resin from trees is runny and sticky, so it's easy for small animals and insects to get stuck. In the right conditions it will harden and turn into amber, meaning that it's possible to see things today that died millions of years ago, such as these Triassic mites.

You Will Need:
- BLACK PAPER • SCISSORS • PENCIL
- PERMANENT MARKER • WHITE CRAFT GLUE • YELLOW PAINT • PAINTBRUSH
- PLASTIC SANDWICH BAG • GLUE STICK

1. Fold a piece of black paper in half and draw a circle shape on one side.

2. Use scissors to cut the circle out of both layers of paper at the same time.

3. Mix the white craft glue with some yellow paint.

4. Draw the mite on one side of the plastic bag using the permanent marker and paint the glue mixture onto the other side. Leave it to dry.

5. Glue the plastic in the middle of the two black sheets. Glue the black sheets together.

Did You Know?
The oldest piece of amber that has been found is 320 million years old!

FLYING ICAROSAURUS

Icarosaurus lived 200 million years ago in the Triassic period. These winged creatures looked like modern day lizards. They didn't use their wings to fly but to glide around for short periods of time.

You Will Need:

- TWO PIECES OF PAPER
- PAPER SCRAPS • SCISSORS
- COLORED PENCILS • GLUE STICK

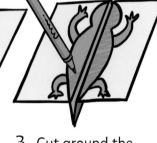

1. Start with one paper in a landscape position and fold in half, then fold another small portion.

2. Partially open the paper and draw on a lizard body.

3. Cut around the lizard body and color in with pencils.

4. Start with the other paper in a portrait position and fold in half, then fold again as in Step 1.

5. This time open the paper up completely and make the wings. Color in before gluing them onto the body.

6. Make a tail from scraps of paper and glue it to the body.

DINOSAUR PUZZLE

CAN YOU FIND THE ANSWERS TO THESE QUESTIONS?

1. How many palm trees can you spot?

2. Which of the lava trails reaches the T. rex?

3. How many craters are there on the meteor?

4. Where is the second dinosaur hiding?